Military satellites better than nonmilitary ones

By: Ehsan Azarang

Introduction

If there has been lot of time from sending messages by drum voice in nomadic tribes until emerging telegraph, but there has not been such long interval between telegraph and satellites era. During this time, the quick communication technology has been transformed extensively after combining the micro electronic and communication. The satellites are the advanced communicative devices that may be launched to space by missile or shuttle and position in orbit, control the surface, depth of earth and other planets by their eyes and ears from the height. And they provide the useful information for earth bases, almost in all fields. They are in military and unmilitary types. Satellites make possible to establish connections between countries, even continents and create the cooperative fields among various countries in various fields. Satellite technology as a main branch in spatial researches, has very huge situation in various fields of communication, geomorphology, military, nonmilitary and aerology. Despite their low lifetime and because of relying on all physical and engineering knowledge of human and the need that may be felt for them especially about communication field, satellites have been grown quickly and have became an inseparable component of human life. Growths of TV satellites and telephone communication by satellite, mix this device with human life as an nonmilitary one. The primary satellites in compared with today systems were initial systems. Satellites

3

that had been launched to space were small, had low lifetime and low capacity for scientific, military and specialized applications. But today satellites have been improved by eliminating of their problems. We use of satellite every day without recognizing its value. Forecasting the weather, condition of next day, incidents news that may be occurred across the world, remote telephones and Internet communication system all depend on satellites. The international, commercial and industrial sectors exchange millions of information in one second by using of satellite communication network. The intelligence satellites are capable to photograph from movements of missile bases and army through military bases throughout the world. The engineering satellites depict earth map and farmers, miners, construction engineers and foresters use of these maps. Detectors satellite help to pilots, discoverers, navigators and passengers to find their path. Most important, millions of people watch TV programs that have been sent by satellites in orbit with using of satellite receivers.

Position of the satellite in synchronically orbit[1] means that observer can observe the satellite constantly in one stable point in the sky. Satellites from this 35870 kilometers space (22291miles) can receive, sustain and resend radio signals. A receiver on the earth can cover the whole of world by 3 satellites. The more time spend the cost of satellite services on

---

[1] Geostationary orbit

the earth will be cheaper. The Result is that satellites would be cheapest and most suitable ways for sending information in distant spaces, especially if the information targets receivers that are not always in a single place. But today the military satellites are constantly advancing and changing. The information principles express that first, information should be valid and second, today information is better then yesterday information. So satellite plays an extensive role in military program of a country, so that information has became as component of a military operation. We can control a war and drive it toward our goals by extensive using of modern information equipments like satellites. The military commanders can target the sensitive and predetermined goals by using of attained information from various resources especially satellites, from beginning of war with immediate and correct planning, making decisions and step in which path they tend to. The Role of military satellites in securing of correct information, using of satellite images in land, maritime and air operations, its extensive application in receiving of intelligence information and its application in battle, indicate the importance of satellite in current and future era. One of the former Generals of American air force and former commander of US spatial unit said: in the future that forces will be decreased and limited, we will rely on space more and the satellite systems always will play first role in the stage. This structure will constantly transform the world military balance.

One of the French authors wrote about role of satellites: using of height and controlling the enemy actions and behaviors is considered as an art in war like controlling the enemy in past eras. From the first control towers to balloon eras and finally advanced aircrafts,the Human has known that observing from distance means anticipation and this sometimes lead to options of death or live. Now today, not only satellites make easy the using of equipments for commanders by providing correct, tactical and strategical information but also inform them about situation and capability of enemy and climate. This information are very useful in mapping fields like mountains, highways situations, railways and etc. meanwhile they provide information for commanders about food, fuel and water provision resources that each one has a special impact in war operation. Awareness about weakness and strength of enemy, its movements and familiarity with enemy equipments can assist commanders too much. The scientific advances at new age have transformed human lifestyles extensively and give new dimensions to human social life. Today human has opened their path toward world of technology and employed new technical methods for dominating and overcoming on nature and even their peers. invention of these methods, has created the new steps. Modern and sophisticated technology of contemporary age is often emerged by peaceful objectives, but unfortunately some jobbers use of this technology for unjustifiable applications. One of these advances is capturing the space around the earth by human. One of the most important inventions of human in 20 century is satellite. The satellite is result of efforts during years and is the technical advancement peak of human. Because satellites in nonmilitary and military problems have found extra applications and have great evolutions, verifying this application and their resulted evolutions is one of the substantial requirements of strategic studies. Research at this regard, have been conducted by quick investigation about knowledge and power in the past ages until now. Realizing that ages of hunting, farming and industry have been past and today is knowledge age as power tool, as today success in every field need to capability and knowledge. In this research, it has been tried to avoid from complex technical problems and all things has been explained in simple words. Likewise, this research has been translated into English and French, thus some words may not have real meaning after translation.

History of Satellite and satellite launchers

The satellite era have been started on 4th October of 1957. When Soviet Union sent the SPUTNIK to the space. The news sent to throughout of world at 14 o clock in Moscow time and surprised all world people, specially the Americans. One 2 steps Russian missile positioned the satellite in the orbit that its nearest point to earth was 220 kilometers and far point was 947 kilometers. time that satellite could rotate around the earth was 90 minutes. The protection cone shape coating and the latest floor along with SPUTNIK delivered the missile to orbit and at first 3 artificial objects rotated around the world. Scientists called the step in which missile reached to orbit "alpha 1" the satellite "alpha 2" and protected cone shape coating "alpha3". This satellite carries a small radio receiver and an apparatus for measuring the space temperature. After 90 days rotating and sending radio signs to the earth, It was slumped in earth atmosphere and it was burned and destroyed like a shooting stone. In 3th November of 1957 1 month later then launching the SPUTNIK1, Russians surprised the entire world by launching SPUTNIK 2 to space. This 508 kilograms satellite had a substantial difference with SPUTNIK 1.it just had 84 kilograms and it was first time that a being fly to space. Russians sent a dog in a closed room to space and check all of its vital actions, reactions during 7 days and finally they couldn't return it to earth and dog died at same room.

But the Americans work on transporting missile while launching of Russian satellites. by ordering the president, this scheme stopped temporary and the Americans prepare for launching the EXPLORER[2]. Thus the first American satellite known as EXPLORER that its weight was only 17/3 kilograms was launched to space at 31 th January of 1958. This satellite carries various scientific equipments and sent some information about exist beams and lights in space to the earth. thus the satellite discovered ionic Irradiation belt around the earth so it was called VAN ALLEN belt in the glory of well known physician JAMES VAN ALLEN. He predicted the existence of this belt .at 17 th march of 1958, VANGUARD satellite that belonged to maritime force of America was launched. After this era, 2 superpower countries and other ones launched thousands of satellites. The new age of spatial technology started but which country invented the missile, which is the main tool of launching a satellite? Not Americans nor Russians invented the missile but china invented it .Chinas firstly invented gunpowder, then make fire game tools and torpedo by gunpowder. in fact, torpedo was small type of missile. Chinese used of torpedo in wars to frighten enemy. Torpedo were fabricated this way, they poured some gunpowder in a tube that its top is closed and

---

[2] it really proved that its name is deserved for it

they didn't close other top and lit it by tinder. This action caused firing the gunpowder ,collecting the gas inside tube and gas wend out through the side that was not closed and torpedo threw to air in contrary direction. ISSAC NEWTON in 1687 considered a rule in PRINCIPIA book which this action is justified scientifically. During those years, the method of fabricating the gunpowder and torpedo were moved to west. Europeans used of gunpowder more in artillery.

At the end of 18th century, English battled with Indian soldiers in India. Indians used of missile for throwing stone toward English. One of the English officers called WILLIAM CONGREVE by observing this action thought that they could throw the bullets to more distance by making the suitable missiles and destroys more the impact of artillery ballets. He designed the better missiles that were used in early of 19 century by English maritime and land forces in battling with their enemies. one of these countries was the united states of America. Battle between England and US lasted from 1812 to 1814. In 1814 England forces surrounded the McHENRY military base in Baltimore port in Maryland state. Although they did not win the war but except bullet they also threw missile.

In this conditions nobody thought to travel to space by missile. Of course 40 years before NEWTON, a French story writer called CYRANO DE BERGERAC represented several ways for traveling to moon. Most ways of him were stupid and incredible. But in one way he had wrote about using missile but nobody mattered him.

After years no scientist had cited missile as a device for traveling from the earth to outside space. In 1895 KONSTANTIN EDUARDOVICH TSIOLKOVSKY the Russian physician studied the matter of traveling with missile from earth to space. He thought the satellite or any object that want to travel to space should be thrown by missile. but he did not think to launching missile by gunpowder but he accepted the liquid fuel as appropriate one. The liquid fuels had 2 advantages then gunpowder 1- its power was more then gunpowder 2- because of liquidity they could be controlled easily and their speed can be decreased or increased by adjusting the entry quantity to fuelling place.

Today liquid fuel are used in most of transporters. For example, cars and airplanes use of petrol. Although petrol should be mixed with air oxygen for producing energy in these tools but because they move in earth atmosphere, there will be no problem.

The problem will be changed when devices want to pass from vacuum in space. There is no air in outside space and the missile that wants to move in vacuum should have required oxygen. The oxygen is transformed to liquid in order to decrease its volume because of cooling. TSIOLKOVSKY who comprehended the matter, wrote some articles in an aviation magazine in 1903 there was considered many details about missile fabrication. Not only he discussed about liquid fuel and oxygen but also about spatial stations and survival and living in space and very other notes. He had said the earth is cradle of human but he cannot live in cradle forever. Despite he planned the way of missile working but never tried to fabricate such device. he died in 19 September of 1935. It has written on his grave stone: the human can never commit to live in the earth. The first person who fabricated the missile with liquid fuel was an American scientist called ROBERT HUTCHINGS GODDARD. He was born in WORCESTER one of the Massachusett cities. he was interested in studying on missile and he registered 2 inventions about missile until 1914 . He wrote a book in 1919 which there was explained the missile and its using way. his ideas was very similar to TSIOLKOVSKY ones. After that GODDARD fabricated missiles with liquid oxygen and petrol fuel He tested his first missile in 16th march of 1926 in AUBURN in Massachusett. GODDARD fired and missile rose 56 meters and its speed reached to 96/5 kilometers in one hour. Of course it was not considered as a good speed but it indicated that the missile engine works. GODDARD decided to fabricate larger missile. he could receive money from SMITHSON institution in Washington and flied the larger missile in January of 1929 near the WORCESTER. The missile was quicker and flied higher then first missile. It was accompanied with a camera, pressure gauge and thermometer. it was the first missile that could attain some information from atmosphere by carrying scientific equipments. But GODDARD were faced with a problem, people knew him as a stupid person. New York times even derided him and called him as a silly person. one day one of GODDARD's missile flied with the loud voice. The neighbors informed police and firefighters. Goddard was ordered to stop his missile tests.

But one of Goddard's friend supported him and gave money to him. By using of his money, GODDARD could establish a laboratory in a distant place. He started to fabricate the large missile there and tested most of his inventions that was the result of advanced and novel missile fabrication there. For example one of them was fabrication of multisteps missile that rose to higher height and did not carry all fuel and oxygen. GODDARD were dubbed as "spatial flight Christopher Columbus "it is true for him. GODDARD registered 214 inventions about missile fabrication before death. From 1930 to 1935, He could launch missiles that reached to 885 kilometers speed in 1 hour and 2/4 kilometers height. Despite disregarding to his efforts continued, It can be said that nobody was aware from his works. The American government even did not encourage him. But condition in German was different. There, some scientists were trying to fabricate missile or thought to go to space. For this regard, the spatial travels association started its work in 1927 in German. One of its first members was a youth called WILLY LEY. He introduced other youth named WERNER VON BRAUN to association. The association could fabricate 85 missiles with liquid fuel and launched it to space. On contrary of GODDARD who worked lonely, the association started to cooperate with various people and collecting important contributions. Adolph Hitler reached to power in 1933 in Germany. Hitler who had combative and dictatorship thoughts, considered missiles as good weapons. so he supported from spatial travels association.

In 1936, in northwest of Germany, there established a secret site for missile tests. The German government contributed the massive money to missile making and research program of von braun. In 1938 Von Braun could made some missiles that flied 17 kilometers. At the beginning of world war Von Braun started to fabricate more powerful missiles[3] so that they could carry explosive material and collide rightly to targets that were located in enemy lands. their speed must be so that would not be slumped by enemy anti air artilleries and aircrafts.

Germans could not fabricate diverse weapons but one of the most important ones was an automated aircraft named V-1. von braun invented some better missiles that were in real shape and could move quicker then voice speed. They were called V-2. Germans launched 4300 missiles totally. But world people were very fortunate that Hitler army attained V2

---

[3] launchers

missiles late. The V2 missiles encouraged the US and Soviet Union to fabricate missile. Each country were frightened from the power of other country and tried to attain most advanced weapons. While capturing Germany, both countries tried to trap the missiles makers too much. The US could employ Von Braun to its service. After war, both countries tried to make larger and better missiles. In 1950 some giant missiles were fabricated so that the V-2 in compared with them was like as a toy. Finally both US and Soviet Union could be successful in making missiles that were able to guide to each point of the world and collide there. The missiles had not the usual explosive material like v-2 any more but they could carry the nuclear bomb. No doubt, using of missile for war were not in GODDARD and TSIOLKOVSKY minds. They wanted missiles for exploring in outside space.

Of course the missiles were used in science purposes too. While capturing Germany, the Americans attained to some V-2 and launched them for scientific research. The missiles carry apparatus for registering the atmosphere specifications instead of inflammable material. One of them was in 183/4-kilometer height that is several times more then balloons height. In 1949 the Americans put a small missile on top of a V-2 missile. when v-2 reached to maximum of its height, the small missile worked and rose to 386 kilometers height.

Russians who did not like to fall behind their opponent, made so efforts in space missiles and also satellites. Of course other countries were interested in spatial matters to some extent. For example an article by ARTHUR C .CLARKE were published in British WIRELESS WORLD magazine about stable satellites with earth in 1945. The British engineer had explained some communication satellites and their position in space very clear and apparent on his time. But as described before, finally Russians sent first satellite to space. After launching the VANGUARD, EXPLORER, SPUTNIK satellites, both US and Soviet Union launched more intelligence and scientific satellites. But there is no doubt that US launched more scientific satellites to space. In 1958 the communication satellite known as SCORE was launched by US air force. This satellite published a taped message from president of US on Christmas day. It was first time that voice of human is sent from space. On that time, the first rotating satellite called as DISCOVERER 1was launched in pole. This satellite was an introduction until 1960 the first aerologic satellite known as TIROS circuit in orbit. This satellite was a TV one with indicator system of infrared rays. In 1962 a non-governmental satellite known as TELSTAR1 was launched. This satellite transferred the TV programs on Atlas Ocean for first time.

In 1964 the first communication satellite that was really static than earth was launched. its name was SYNCOM3. its first series could not survive on its orbit and the second series had not been considered static because of a 30 degrees deviation than earth in its orbit. But the satellite deviation in its orbit was 0 degree. So it was positioned in a fixed location than earth during days and nights. During years the INTELSAT organization were formed. The organization was established for spatial cooperation between countries and accomplishment of shared projects. Initially it had 19 members. The Soviet Union in next days established the INTERSPUTNIK organization. It was similar to INTELSTA organization and had 9 members firstly.

But the first military communication satellites of the world was launched to space in 1965.the satellite was called LES 1, was positioned in an orbit with 2800 kilometers height than earth. The satellite was very advanced and modern at its time and same year, the first communication satellite of the world with same name was launched to space by INTELSAT organization. Of course other name of this project was EARLY BIRD. The satellite carried 240 telephone orbits or a TV channel. After that, the US and Soviet Union launched very satellites. But this commission considered a rule as open skies by decision that adopted to increas the launchers volume. Based on this rule, each organization that act in law framework and people interests, can have a satellite. Consequently, the spatial companies like HUGHES and WESTERN UNION developed their work. From that time, numerous satellites has been positioned in orbit which some of them are military and some of them are nonmilitary. Of course other countries have not fell behind the competition and try to be advanced in this field.

What is the satellite?

Satellite:

If an object rotates around a planet, it will be called moonlet. If human fabricates that object, it will be called satellite. Satellites like planets and moonlets has moving and situational movements. Satellite is one of the most expensive machine slabs in the world. But fabricating its slabs in lighter and smaller dimensions will make it less expensive.

Satellites shapes:

the geometric shape of satellites never limits because they move outside of atmosphere and they can be made in any shape. But for more efficiency it is used of 4 main plans: cannon shape satellites, sphere shape satellites, cane shape satellites and cube shape satellites. Among them, it is used of cannon and cube shape most of others. Height of the cannon shape satellites is from   1 to 5 meters. The normal size of cube satellites is 1/8 meter. but some of them may be longer and even be in car size.

Energy generating in satellites:

there is an energy provision apparatus in satellites, which is guided by a radio sender from the earth, and it is always active. A huge part of this apparatus are compromised from the solar batteries that they get the required energy from sun.

The solar cells are placed on wings that are installed on the satellite sides. The wings are called solar panels. Of course in some of satellites the solar cells are installed on satellite. The cannon satellites are from this type. The more solar panel is larger, the electrical energy in each satellite will be provided more. Of course it is used of atomic small generators for some long-term missions, which its site is far from the earth. Satellites by their size consume much electrical energy because each satellite with due to its function is equipped to various tools of research identification, photography measurement, and all type of advanced telecommunication devices and computers. And these equipments need to energy. So the more provider apparatus of energy in satellites is powerful, its efficiency will be more. As mentioned before fabricating the light and small parts the launching less expensive. But other advantages of light and small satellite parts are saving fuel and side costs. But the steel coating of satellites should be very durable because it should tolerate the extreme thermal modulations. If satellite is positioned in earth shadow, it will be cold so that its part noise. On contrast, against sun light its steel body get warm so there will be always possibility that exist tools in satellite get cold or warm so that they breakdown. Because of not existence of air in space, adjusting temperature to thermal exchange method with environment is not possible. But with irradiation methods, the temperature can be changed. for this reason, the satellites are coated with material that are thermal insulator and reflect the reached beams.

Satellite lifetime:

Satellite lifetime depends on orbit shape and orbit distance from the earth. The more height of satellite moving orbit is, the satellite will be survived in orbit longer. it is also tried that the satellite orbit be oval near circle and its movement path be outside the atmosphere in order to avoid from preventing and overlapping impact of earth atmosphere Because the air resistance in more thick layers of atmosphere, can cause extreme overlapping and even burning the satellite.

Receiving and sending information:

Radio signs guide a satellite. The signs are beams that send from dish shape air aerials or established aerials in land station on the earth toward satellite. This type of information sending is called land to air communication. Satellites also send beams that carry the information like its position in space, its battries situation, calculation or photos to same land or other stations. Most of satellites are equipped to automated receivers and senders. The receiver and sender system sustain the received signs of an earth station and telecommunicate it by a sender aerial to earth station. So the telecommunication satellites sustain radio signs and send it to distance.

Orbit

Satellites are rotating in a closed path that is called orbit. The earth centers are located in orbit plate. In other words, orbit and earth center are in same plate. Most of orbits are oval and earth centers are located in one focuses of this oval. Locating satellite in orbit is justified so that every thing that moves in direct line finally will be affected by gravity force. Satellites tend to move in direct line but the earth gravity try to fall it down. satellite fall down but never return to earth because earth surface is curve and is far from satellite. So satellite continues its movement in this curve path and rotates around earth continually. Satellites are different by locating in orbits. The satellites, which are in downer orbit, can provide some standard photos and send them by capsule with parachute to earth. As there are satellites that provide images in real time (when event occur) and at this moment send it to earth digitally. Higher then such satellites, there are some satellites in middle orbit of earth between 1000 to 10000 miles that detect the radar of other countries and determine its frequency,range,power and its other specifications exactly. Other type of such satellites works fourfold. (Like intelligence satellite KH12). 2 night identification satellites and 2 other satellites guide the day identification. Thus these satellites can take photos from each place on the earth during several minutes after receiving photos order in real time. For preserving satellites in a fixed orbit and change its site, some equipments have been fabricated that are for directing, modifying and detecting satellites.

The review of satellites system engineering

Designing the satellite communication system is a complex action that need to common work in diverse knowledge. First problem in designing is satellite. Satellites should be light as possible as and use of minimum energy. Putting 1-kilogram mass in each orbit can be very expensive. Electricity production for space ship moving are required to weight tolerance and solar cells surface. In military and nonmilitary satellites there is a very important factor and it is communication capacity. So for this regard, satellite should be able to carry very communicative channels. Likewise because the launching and satellites are so expensive, the spatial satellites should be able to continue its work in extreme vacuum environment without any action for preserving. in this conditions, satellites sometimes are exposed to extensive warm rotation ,irradiation constant bombing, sub nuclear bits bombing and small shooting stone and it should continue its work after all of these steps. If in designing a satellite, all of these problems is solved, there would be problem again and it is the technology evolution. Because of quick and unexpected evolutions of technology and especially communication technology, satellites should be designed so that at first they are flexible for every technical change in their designing use of most modern and latest technology. Other consideration in satellites designing is distance between earth and satellite. Assuming that satellite is located in an orbit that its distance with earth is 36000 kilometers. For communication between earth and satellite a signal should pass from this space once to satellite in convergent orbit. And it should definitly return from this pass. The suitable decline with space quadrate is too high and the decline will be increased in frequencies higher then 10 giga hertz. This process is called decline caused by precipitation. The resolution for decreasing this signal decline is using of strong senders and aerials. In sending signal from earth, despite expensive equipments, the large aerials and senders can be used. But in sending signal from satellite so earth, the aerial size and sender power is limited by what satellite can carry and electricity that can be produced for it. The received signals are very weak, it means weaker then exist signals in each type of communication system. The result is than aerial usage, disruption of receiver and sender power should be considered. Even after finishing these works, depending on technical and economical limitations of hardware, the engineers try to design the satellites communication software. Likewise a lot of works should be done in designing for discovering and correcting the sending errors. Because in military satellites plus the signal-sustaining problem, there is a problem in encoding the signals. Multi purposes Accessing is other problem. A military or nonmilitary satellite can has numerous users who may be dispersed in a country or even continent. In military satellite for advancing the military objective and in nonmilitary and commercial satellite for maximizing income, these satellites should be able to service to most of users who can be changeable efficiently. Finally the land stations problems is considered. The stations should be very reasonable for their unmilitary users and be very safe for military users. But both in unmilitary stations and military stations, there is a common aspect and that is, they should be very powerful and complex for effective and efficient communication with its satellites. stations should be adapted with many lawful appropriates and governmental licensing. They should be able to find their satellites quickly and keep their communication with them even in unexpected changes.

How satellites fly to space?

Satellites are launched to space by missile or shuttle with driving force like energy sources and converter engine and they located in a certain orbit and moved.

There should be haste more then the earth gravity one for launching an object from the earth gravity scope. As human consume energy for walking, the transporters should encounter with air resistance and overlapping too and finally they loose some energy.

In movement of launcher objects, the action and reaction rule of Newton is true. Based on this rule every action has a reaction. For example, based on this rule if someone in a sled and in a flat path throws back 2 bricks he goes forward a little. But if he throws back 10 bricks at it situation will go forward more so that the sled moving is a reaction due to throwing bricks. Other example, if we have a balloon full of wind and release it, the air will be exited from it and the balloon will be moved in contrary of exist air because the pressure inside balloon is much then environmental pressure. It is true in missile combustion capsule. Of course the operation is adjusted and controlled by gas exiting and other equipments. When the balloon is released it will be moved adrift. But the tube of gas exiting is fabricated in missile so that drive it in a controlled direction. The more is the gas pressure in every second that is exited from missile to outside and speed of gas exiting, the advancing force of missile will be more. the missile that carry the spatial satellites should have high gravity fleeing haste in order to leave the earth. Missiles for reaching to such haste need to high energy. But by operation of launching in special geographical points the energy can be reduced. when the missile is on the earth because of earth rotating movement, it tends to move in western to eastern direction meanwhile if the earth rotation speed near the equator is more then other points so when missile is launched in western to eastern direction, the more launching sites that is near to equator the missile will need to less driving power and less energy will be spent. and finally the missile can transfer the more expensive burden to orbit. For this reason, the Russians missile are launched from BAIKONOUR base in ghazaghistan with 46 north latitude and the American missiles are launched from CAPECANAVERAL spatial station in Florida with 28 north latitude. likewise the European missile launching bases, KOUROU in France gooyan are in better geographical position than both Russians and American bases because that is located in 5 north latitude.

How does satellites reach to their orbit?

The satellites are located in highest part of transporters missile and begin their journey to a certain orbit. The missiles are often comprised from floors or steps that each one has a single engine. When the fuel of one step is depleted the empty capsule will be separated from missile and next step will be started. The more missile height from earth is its movement angle will be more inclined as finally the missile will be advanced in a parallel surface with above layers of earth atmosphere. Before separating the last tank of missile fuel from satellite, it should be reached to appropriate speed for moving in specified orbit. So missiles deliver the satellites directly to specified orbit. Some of them also deliver the satellites firstly to orbit that is considered as a temporary place for stopping or final launching site for satellite. satellites that are located in such orbits known as transferring orbits, are risen by driving system toward other orbit and medium and finally toward their orbit in order to perform their tasks there. The satellites that moving from an orbit to other one in the space is called orbital moving. 2 stimulus forces move satellite from one orbit to higher one. First stimulus is received when satellite is located in nearest orbit point than earth and second stimulus is received when the satellites is located in far orbit point then earth. The satellite should be reached to certain speed and proportional with its orbit height in order not to exit from the orbit and not to slump. The speed is somehow that balance between earth gravity force and gravitation that can bring out the satellites from earth around orbit (centrifugal). So the satellites should have a moving direction and certain site in space for example in order to receive the sending news from land aerials. But in some satellites missions it is required that the satellites moving orbit to be changed. But how do these forces work? The centrifugal direction is toward outside from earth center. The force affect on satellites which is moving on the earth around orbit so that want to throw them outside of orbit and the points away from earth. The earth gravity force acts on contrary of centrifugal and attract satellites down earth. The earth gravity force exerts on all objects and it is also known as gravity stable. The centrifugal and gravity should interact so that the satellite don't fell down or disappeared on space forever. While launching missile, 7 g gravity will exert on it. It means when a missile that carries human is launched, it tolerates the force 7 times more then its weight. But while launching the missile, the condition get easier because the speed will be increased gradually and the haste will not be enhanced suddenly. By controlling satellite speed, the inhibition capabilities of such forces can be prevented.

The special equipments are designed for satellite in order to adjust and identify its direction and position on orbit by SENSORS and special guiders. Therefore a 3 axis guidance apparatus and rotating guidance help to satellite to be able to survive in space in a stable point and likewise it can be rotated around its central axis. Each year a lot of satellites are launched to space that each one has especial function. It is invented a lot of advancing systems and various plans for each kind of these satellites that each one are comprised from exact and complex components.

Launching equipments

Most of satellites, which are launched, located in orbit by missile called ELVS. The TITAN, DELTA,ATLAS missiles are belonged to US and ENERGIA ,PROTON are belonged to Russia, LONG MARCH is belonged to china and H Seri is for Japan and ARIANE missile are belonged to Europe. The fabrication of such missiles is very expensive because they cannot be recovered and would be destructed after launching or would be suspended on space. The only launcher missile that can be recovered is SPACE SHUTTLE by exclusive name as STS that is belonged to US.

Launching market

The US has increased the long-term policy of ELVS launching and has relied on STS merely. This has led to granting ELVS to private sector in the US because the government has sold many ELVS equipments to non-governmental users. The European company known as ARIAN has spread its ELVS launching too much and it has become as a rigid competitor for US in marketing for unmilitary launchings. Russians also do their especial work by launching and don't care to commercial market too much. But Japan and china are entering to market and launch some Asian satellites.

Choosing the launcher

The owner of an unmilitary satellites like a telecommunication satellites has 3 better options among launchers: 1- the American ELVS specially DELTA 2- STS 3- ARIAN systems.

Each one has its especial fans but none can be known as more reasonable or technical than others. For this reason, in designing satellites, they are fabricated so that they can be compatible with 2 or 3 launchers. The GSTAR satellite is from this type.

All of launching types has its advantages and disadvantages. For example shuttle can carry more burden and tolerate less gravity while launching, it can be inspected in space and it is repairable before positioning in orbit. But its major disadvantage is that has more limitations by safety for satellites designers than ELVS by launching from equipment that carry human. For example STS launching satellites should not use of inflammable material, and should has STS standards by safety.

ARIAN use of its capability to attaining movement orbit with little bias by southern launching site. ARIAN as a equipment that don't carry human exert some less safety limitations for satellites designers. But it cannot be inspected on space clearly. DELTA is older then ARIAN and has less power then it. But it uses of a sustained technology. Like DELTA, ARIAN also has problems of carrying and not carrying of human against STS. Likewise DELTA cannot attain to movement orbit with little bias angle that is offered by ARIAN through an American launching. Thus this question is raised that how long DELTA can be survived. The cost differences between launchers may be more important then technical matters. Although a large of DELTA launchers has been assigned to private sector in the US but NASA also launches ELVS and it has never certain price for such launchings. Although the prices with best estimation are determined for launching contracts, but all of governmental launching costs in the US should be compensated And from this view, the customer has less power in payment time and payment way. This policy is also true for STS. the ARIAN has an advantage here. ARIAN spatial company as a private company can sign up crucial commercial contracts with users. Likewise it is able to offer the more flexible programs openly about time and way of payment.

The missile fuel

For missile movement, it is used of fuels that due to its inflammation, the missiles move very quickly and can flee from earth gravity. The missiles that move with chemical fuels usually are categorized to 3 groups:

1- The chemical missiles with liquid fuel: in chemical missiles with liquid fuel, the oxidation materials are stored in separate tanks in liquid. The fuel material usually is consisted of liquid hydrogen or similar compounds and oxidation material is usually liquid.

2- The chemical missiles with solid fuel: in such missiles, the oxidation material and fuel is already mixed and converted to solid and don't need atmosphere oxygen.

3- The chemical missiles with bred fuel: third type of missiles fuel is bred type in which fuel material is stored as solid fuel and oxidative material is stored as liquid.

What orbit is for satellites movements?

The satellites are rotating on a certain orbits around the earth. Some of the orbits have circle shape and others have oval shape. Their height from earth is also different. Other difference of such orbits is in angular declivity, which they form with equator. This difference indicates that from which angle, the satellites pass from equator. Satellites can move on orbit that is crossing from equator or on pole circle and include north and south poles. An orbit can be biased than equator. Selecting of moving orbit for each satellite depends on type of functions that are assigned to satellite. generally the main orbits around the earth are :

1- The land orbit-stable (GEO)/ this orbit is almost oval shape and are located in 36000 kilometers height beyond equator. The satellites that are moving on such orbit is rotating around earth per 24 hours and for this reason, it is located on a stable point than earth surface. (In front of stable point of earth) the telecommunication satellites, TV satellites and special satellites for observing and mapping of earth are launched to this orbit.

34

2- The oval shape orbit(EO)/ the nearest point of this orbit is 200 kilometers and far point is about 40000 kilometers away from earth. When the satellite approach to peak point(the far point of orbit than earth) its speed get lower and when it advance to apsis(nearest point of orbit than earth) it will move quicker. Most of military satellites are moving on this orbit.

3- The polar orbit (PO) distance from this orbit to earth is minimum 400 kilometers and maximum 1000 kilometers. The satellites for geomorphology researches, guidance and directing satellites and observing earth satellites use of such orbit.

4- The high height orbit (HEO)/ distance of this orbit to earth is minimum 10000 kilometers and maximum 20000 kilometers. The satellites guidance and directing of ships and airplanes use of this oval shape orbit.

5- Low height orbit (LEO)/ distance of this orbit to earth is minimum 400 and maximum 1000 kilometers. This orbit is nearly circle shape. Aerology, observing and mapping, research and scientific and human carrier satellites are rotating on this orbit.

What is the major function of satellites? What is sepratibilitiy?

It was considered exaggerative news about satellites capabilities in initial steps of attaining human to satellites and this caused no one feel secure after publishing the news of intelligence satellites launching. On contrast other persons knew any accessing to information of other countries from space as forbidden and considered it as tool for psychological warfare by superpowers. But after short time, part of secrets that was related to this technology was exposed. We refer to performance and capabilities of satellites in following:

The major function of satellites is included recording information by receiving electromagnetic waves. From such waves, the human eyes can observe just 0.4 to 0.7 micron. But until now the human could use of a considerable amount of this spectra by using of devices and equipments. Some of satellites can photograph from earth by photography systems and using of films with special sensibility and lens.

Satellites also photograph by using of radar systems. The satellites that photograph by using of radar system are able to receive information even in cloudy weather and at night. Some satellites record reflective waves and electromagnetic spectra beams that are irradiated from object by converting of reflective modulations to electrical variations and through digital recording on special strips. But just one thing is important in all of such satellites and that is separability.

The Separability is called as capability to separate and to show smaller objects on the earth clearly by a satellite.

Separability of satellites starts from several millimeters to several kilometers. The LANDSAT satellites had 35 meters separability in non-thermal bands. The SPOT satellites had XS band top and 20 meters of separability, and of course they also had a band with 10 meters separability. The satellites like NOAA had 1100 meters separability while the KEY HOLE 7 had 6 inches separability.

The satellites systems are so capable that not only they can photograph from visible length waves, but also they show phenomenon that have various irradiations in visible bands because of having unique physical problem or chemical combinations. Today the satellites images have mill metric sepratibility and weakness of such system are decreasing day to day and the new equipments are added to them. finally by such capabilities, they will achieve to some results that human cannot access and identify them.

Sometimes a satellite with high sepratability can have efficiency more then what is expected. for example in 1987 an intelligence satellite belonged to US that was located in stable orbit with earth, identified some missed hostages in Lebanon who moved from one building to another. The information recording related to the terrorists was done completely and they were identified easily. Recording the all of such specifications can be done during night, beyond thick clouds and from various heights.

The most important unmilitary satellites and their performance

The unmilitary satellites can be categorized by their functions. Such satellites are very noticeable and they are developing because of 3 advatages: 1- extensive covering2- frequent and durable covering3-lowering the costs. the nonmilitary satellites from the efficiency view are included following satellites:

1-Telecommunication satellites:

With no doubt, one of the most important satellites from the efficiency view for mankind is telecommunication satellite. Hundreds of telecommunication satellites are rotating in earth orbit. Such satellite transfers or sustains the radio signs between places on the earth that they may be far from each other about thousands kilometers. These signs may be indicator of every thing including individual telephone conversation and sent information from faxes e mail, and internet. The telecommunication satellites also broadcast TV and radio programs and send required information to banks and international commercial markets. A modern telecommunication satellite is able to do 50000 telephony conversations and 30 TV channels synchronically. While you are talking with telephone or sending fax, your voice waves or your writings convert to electric sings. In telecommunication network such signs are diffused as digital codes like pulses that turn on and off with high speed. such digital waves are entered to telecommunication network and are sent toward satellite as digital radio signs. Then these radio signs are returned to earth and somewhere to be decoded and as a result of someone who you are talking with is able to hear your voice. Most of telecommunication satellites are in an orbit along with earth. Although they are moving with 11700 kilometers in each hour but when we observe them from the earth, may feel they are in a stable point of space. Therefore such satellites are usable in all time and it is enough that dish aerial is positioned in its direction.

The telecommunication satellite network started its work in 1965 by establishing the organization of satellite international communication known as INTELSAT. About 135 countries are members of this organization and pay for using of 20 networks of the world telecommunication satellite. The live TV news of the world like Olympic Games is broadcasted by telecommunication network of this organization. Telecommunication satellite system is very efficient about extensive, spread, remote and island countries and the ones that are in mountain regions. Establishing the connection with such countries by sending land radio signs is very difficult.

But telecommunication satellites have a weakness and it is their vulnerabilities against information abduction. Because few telecommunication satellites are charged to send part of secret information like defending programs of governments, new inventions and etc. such information are transferred as coded waves by a satellite to a small receiver aerial on the earth in order to prevent from aliens agents to receive and hear them. But apaches bands of secret information disturb sending such radio signs from satellite by airplane or using of a dish aerial that they install it on high towers. Then they decode signs and gain massive wealth by selling the secret information to intelligence organization.

The most important and efficient telecommunication satellites of the world are included: EUTELSAT that is established by European spatial organization and cover Europe regions from Iceland to turkey. AUSAT that is consisted from 3 old telecommunication satellites and 2 new telecommunication satellites cover whole of Australian continent. BRAZILSAT is very efficient because of spread rainforest and extensive swamp regions in Brazil. INSAT that covers India and Asian southeastern countries and Indian Ocean. And ASIA SAT that is located in center of china, this satellite network covers 30 countries that include half of world population.

2-TV satellites:

Most of satellites are communicated with 1 or more established stations on the earth surface. The land stations are equipped to large dish aerials that their diameter is about 18 meters or more. Such aerials are capable to receive the

41

weakest radio sings which the home satellites aerial have not such efficiency. Method work is that the TV and radio programs are sent to sender center of land station from TV and radio studio and the center send radio signs to specified satellite. After receiving the satellite sustains waves and telecommunicates them to other receiver aerial of land station. Then, land cables transfer radio signs to land broadcasting tower and it send radio signs to under- coverage regions, then normal receiver aerials in homes receive signs easily.

Some of homes receive airwaves from satellite directly. The method is started from early 1980s and it is known as DBS. Initially there were 2 considerable problems in front of such sending method. The sending signs must cover extensive region until more population use of sent programs. And secondly such signs should be very powerful in order to be receivable by cheap and small dish aerials too. Of course for this regard, a decoding device should be installed on TV. during 1990s the new types of solar batteries, automated receiver and sender devices and other equipments were fabricated. And it meant that satellites could send radio sings with more power and cover extensive area.

In 1996 DBS satellites series known as HOTBIRD are launched for European regions that as a result it, people could receive more TV channels, which cover throughout of Europe. Japan, Asian southeastern, Asian southwestern and South American countries are now sustaining the satellite TV programs systems. in the US there are tens of governmental TV channels and hundreds of local TV channels that are receivable by land broadcasting or cable centers. so direct receiving system from satellite or same DBS is less considerable in this country. But during the time, the direct receiving system of satellite TV programs (DBS) has became considerable in this country and is getting popular.

But the TV satellites have a disadvantage and it is their undesirable quality synchronically for all under- coverage area. The area that is covered by a satellite and it sends TV signs there, is called trace. The area that is under coverage of satellites can be shown by lines depiction on a map. There are powerful signs in center of area and received TV images and voices are in high quality. But little by little that we get far from this center we can see the signs as weaker. So around of the center, the voice and image are not with high quality. By using of larger receiver dish aerials, the huger masses of such signs are receivable and the quality of received voice and image can be improved by this way.

3-the detector satellites:

Navigators, discoveres, tourists and passengers found their path by using of compass and calculation of stars, moon, sun. but today we only need to a satellite receiver like GLOBAL POSITIONING SYSTEM (**GPS**) for finding the most difficult paths. the receiver is similar to mobile phone. When turn it on

43

we can find where we are positioned. And it also gives us a map from site that we are in and it informs us about our height from sea and if we are riding a car, it makes us aware about our speed and direction.

Today most of airplanes and ships get help from satellite in order to find their path. the detector satellite system are included 24 satellites at 6 fourfold groups that four satellites of each group move behind each other in a connected orbit and in 20180 kilometers height from earth. The orbits of these 6 groups form angles than each other so that cover all of world points. it means one ship in every point of the world can be aware from its position. but the detector receivers are not only for airplanes or ships, they can be used personally like in cars that are equipped to GPS receiver system. The driver while being aware from his path can observe site map on the screen and choose a path that has less traffic or select the shortest one. A GPS receiver apparatus that receives radio sings at boat, ship or car in any part of the word, at least assigns 4 to 11 satellites in each moment to the device. Of course the apparatus is capable to show the code of satellite that has sent signs. A little time last in order to send radio sings from each satellite to GPS receiver apparatus. Therefore the radio signs of most distant satellites are received later then others. There is installed a small computer on receiver apparatus in order to receive related information and you can find your position by this way.

Most of airplanes, ships and important transporters carry a receiver apparatus called SARSAT. in emergency conditions this sender sends some radio signs that is identified by satellite system called SARSAT "the rescue and explorer satellites". Such satellites receive the related emergency message and then send the exact position of incident and related signs to related centers.

4- Mapping satellites:

When people travel to new location they usually have a map by themselves. The mapping satellites help such people to depict map site. The satellites are equipped to very powerful cameras and are able to observe buildings, farms, roads and natural terrain like hills, cliffs, rivers and lakes as well as ports and ships. These cameras convert light beams that are diffused from anything throughout the earth surface to radio signs and send them to established land stations on the earth. In these stations, the radio signs are converted to image which by helping them, the new maps are depicted and any kind of changes on the earth would be reevaluated.

The first mapping satellite started its work in 1972 by launching LAND SAT to earth orbit. at present, the LAND SAT 4 and LAND SAT 5 are in earth orbit and rotate around the earth 15 times in day. While earth rotates around, such satellites pass from earth while rotating and photograph from it. Each one of the LAND SAT satellites covers an area about

185 kilometers by using of their powerful cameras while rotating. Such cameras are capable to observe objects with 35 meters width. Therefore the satellites can observe a high building or large ship easily. The LAND SAT satellite cameras are able to receive and identify light beams and infrared rays that are visible at night.

Mapping satellite called as SPOT is belonged to Europe and rotates in 830 kilometers height from earth and covers an area with 20-kilometer width. This satellite covers all earth area each 26 days.

The photos that are taken by mapping satellites show various plant areas like Forrest, pine trees, wheat and corn farms. We can be informed from quality growth of agriculture products by using those satellites and this help to farmers to improve quality of their products. But today satellites are not able to identify what is happened in ocean and sea depth exactly. But there is possibility for invention of a satellite type that its sending beams are able to cross water and make us aware from what is in oceans and seas. By that time, such satellites can depict a precise map from seabed, pursue and detect clusters of whales and fishes and identify and indicate the intelligence submarines.

The photos that are taken by mapping satellites make us aware about cliffs and faults in which there may be valuable coal, oil or other mines. Collecting such information from distance is known as "determining from the distance". Some of these photos show the denes in which roaring river are flowing. Such places are very appropriate for building barrier and can use of them for electricity production.

5-the aerologic satellites

Satellites have enhanced our knowledge about weather conditions extensively. As a result, the climate forecasting is performed by aerologic airplane precisely. Millions of world people from farmers to fishers, pilots to captains deal with aerologic reports every day.

Multiple Aerologic satellites inform us about weather conditions. The first series of such satellites known as TIROS started their work in 1960. The satellite is a TV one with infrared rays' indicator system. This satellite alarmed the probability of storm occurrence like whirlwinds before its starting. from 1970 satellites known as NOAA   that are belonged to geographical and ocean national bureau of the US were established on orbits above pole and sent some information about coverage type of clouds, ice and snow on the earth, bergs, temperature, temperature of earth surface and sea surface and air moisture to the earth by using of scientific equipments during 2 days rotating. METEOR TOMS 3 satellites that were positioned in orbit earth in 1991 made world aware about hole in ozone layer that occurs in each spring above Antarctic. If the diameter of hole becomes larger, area residents will be exposed to much infrared rays of sun. And excessive influence of this ray to earth will put in danger the human, plant and all of beings life.

Several aerologic satellites are rotating in convergent orbit than earth. Such satellites are included EUROPE METEA SAT for Europe and Africa area, INDIA SAT for Asia and Indian ocean and U S GOZ satellite that covers pacific, north, south America and Caribbean.

6 - The scientific satellites

When we observe unclouded sky at nighttime and see stars and moon, our eyes just can observe the visible light beams therefore we can not see many beams that are irradiated from space to earth. But satellites are able to identify such beams. the installed equipments in satellites can identify the beams. Installed equipments in satellites can receive the radio waves, infrared, X rays and gamma and universal beams. So satellites send received beams as radio signs to earth, which then would be analyzed by scientists. Most of scientists believe that earth have been created 14 milliards years ago as a result of a big bang. Satellites can help us to find whether such big bang has been occurred or not. Universal explorer satellites known as COBE that were launched in 1989 spent 5 years to discover natural microwaves in space. Scientists believe that the waves of such big bang are still in space.

Hundreds of satellites are rotating in the space which their application is for research. Observatory known as COMPTON

GRO discovers gamma beams and could discover new stars that are born from huge mass of stars dusts. From 1992 the satellites have started research about infrared rays. Such satellites control very hot stars carefully. IRAS satellites also investigated infrared rays in the space. The beams are irradiated from starts that are hot. But they are not so hot that their irradiations would be as visible light.

One of the largest scientific satellites that were launched by DISCOVERY SPACE SHUTTLE in 1990 was HUBBLE. Its height is 13 meters and it width is 4/3 meters and it is rotating in 613 kilometers from earth. Such telescope is very powerful like telescopes that are established on the earth. But its difference with land telescopes is that atmosphere dust and troublemaker beams never make it disable and consequently it can observe distance clearly. After its repairs in 1993, it has sent thousands of wonderful images from planet, stars and galaxies to the earth until now.

The most important military satellites and their performance

The military satellites by their function types can be categorized. But it does not mean that each military satellite has only one function and it can be said that each satellite are comprised from one or more satellites and does it unique function.

The most important military satellites by their efficiency are included:

1-The military telecommunication satellites

The military telecommunication satellites despite having unmilitary satellites characteristics have special equipments that by them can receive encoded voices and messages, decompose them and then give them to military units. Such satellites perform all of secret communications among political units of countries that have satellite technology and want to communicate with their forign ministry and defence ministry across the world. The satellites often rotate in oval orbit higher than earth.

2-the telecommunication intelligence satellites

such satellites remember for us the James Bond movies. Because they make possible the communication between intelligence centers with their various spies that are dispersed throughout the world by very small and tiny receivers like watch, pen and telecommunicate the attained information to other intelligence center in various points of the world.

3- The intelligence satellites for penetrating in information:

function of such satellites is penetrating in telecommunication systems of enemy missiles and receiving required information. These satellites are able to telecommunicate the attained information to central control stations from switching of missile engine until its return to the earth. The satellites send the abducted information to their interpretation centers.

4- The electrical intelligence satellites:

such military satellites generally pursue and determine positions of air defense radars and missile bases and evaluate the power level of enemy sites. The generation of these satellites receives and reports most information and awareness from radar installations. They also record messages by penetrating in military and unmilitary communication systems and then send them to earth center for tapping. Such satellites often rotate in 400 kilometers higher than earth.

5-Alarming intelligence satellites:

Function of alarming intelligence satellites is informing about distant range missiles of enemy and nuclear explosions. Such satellites are equipped to various and precise determiners which they can determine distant range missile by using of infrared rays and the warmth that is caused by engine switching and they are also able to record nuclear explosions and then telecommunicate their results to the earth. Such satellites, plus determination of distant range missiles launching and nuclear explosions and record any atomic interactions up to 100 millions miles in the space. The satellites have thermometers which they perform intelligence operations in 3 wavelengths (infrared rays, violet rays, visible light) and their position are in convergent orbit in 36000 kilometers than earth.

Another function of these satellites is spying the cruise missiles and airplanes, land to land and air to land missiles situation

6-The photographing intelligence satellites

Photographing intelligence satellites are the oldest military ones. They are equipped to all kinds of cameras, which can take clear photos from enemy targets secretly. In images of such satellites, a military person can be distinguished from a nonmilitary person and cars number while moving can be read. They even can determine the year in which coin has been coined. So nothing can flee from their eyes. the photographing intelligence satellites of Soviet Union were called COSMOS series and of course now Russia seldom use them. they are considered as multi missions satellites. Such satellites took their specified photos from strategic centers and targets and sent them to earth by capsules that were equipped to parachute. They were catched by special airplane of Soviet Union in order to be used after analyzing and development. The intelligence photography satellites of the US are consisted of 2 new series. BIG BIRD and advanced series as KEY HOLE. the satellites are equipped to cameras which can take a clear photo from their specified target. The photography cameras of advance satellites BIG BIRD depending on requirement, take color ,white and black and infrared rays images and so night and day, snowing and sunny don't matter for them. Such images are launched by land commanding within earth atmosphere and then would be catched by unique type of transporter airplane(I think C-130) above sea between earth and air. The KEY HOLE satellites telecommunicate their images by computer digits exclusively so that they never would be disturbed electronically and their contents never would be detected. Of course by advancing of technology, all images of such satellites can be telecommunicated to the earth without trouble and with high speed, but these ways are not applicable for important images because of safety weakness.

The Israel photography intelligence satellite is also from HORIZON series that can take very precise photos from Middle East and telecommunicate them.

Age of the satellites is very short since the orbit that the most of intelligence- photography satellites are in, has lowest lifetime, so any satellite that rotates there, may cracked up. as it said before, the satellites that are in lower orbit would be survived less, so their lifetime is very low. the Russian photography – intelligence satellites from 15 days to 2 months and KEY HOLE and BIG BIRD from 5 months to 1 year can be active in their orbit. Of course at present, their lifetime is increasing extremely and the information is changing day to day.

7-The maritime control- intelligence satellites:

The Function of maritime control – intelligence satellites is investigation and pursuit of enemy maritime movements. The most important Russian maritime intelligence satellites are COSMOS series and as it is said before they often use of nuclear reactor and monitor the west military movements in ocean and sea exactly. They also can be survived in the space by their nuclear generators for years until their energy deplete gradually.

The maritime monitoring-intelligence satellites of US from WHITE CLOUD series are often deployed in 700 miles height and they are also known as ALENT electronic intelligence.

Such satellites are able to receive all maritime signs including all radio and radar sending that ships may reflect them.

7-Special satellites for nuclear explosions:

The characteristics of such satellites that are often positioned in 10000 kilometers than earth in comparison with similar ones include having extra sensitive apparatus to detect irradiations by purpose of determining the time and place of nuclear explosions on the earth.

8-The military aerologic satellites:

They are often positioned between 400 to 1000 kilometers height from earth and investigate climate on the earth. The military aerologic satellites have more advanced technology then nonmilitary ones. They inform various services about weather interactions regularly and it is their main application. Such satellites have 2 separate missions while peace: supporting from photography – intelligence satellites and performing part of aerologic researches.

Anti satellite weapons

Some of countries that have advanced spatial technology, use a spatial technology type for creation of electronic orbits in order to disturb, make parasite or sabotage of enemy. The anti satellite weapons are included laser, and bit beam (including electron and proton atoms which they threw away bits with light speed) and there is another type of anti satellite weapons that is launched by hunting airplane (like F15).

Role of satellites in providing the strategic information

Today satellites are considered as most strong and exact observers in world scale so that they depending on their type can observe smallest object to largest one (like earth planet).

Countries that access to satellite information are able to analyze all power factors in a country since the industry, roads, agriculture products , Mines, and resources like uranium and oil never can be hidden from spatial eyes. They can monitor the military readiness of a country too. Pre awareness about country troubles (like wheat farming in Soviet union) can make enemy ready for misbalancing the economy of specified country. Awareness about oil potential sites and valuable mines in third world countries can encourage the large and major companies to attend in exploring negotiations in specified country.

Based on experts forecasting, in next decade, thousands of satellites with high sepratibility will be launched to the space. Although by the time, few countries will not be able to use of the satellites information but they will be highly lost because of disability in information competition.

Using of nonmilitary satellites in providing strategic information get significance every day because of enhancing the separability. But if strategic information is obtained whether by military satellites or nonmilitary satellites is very important in national level, and most of countries that have satellite unique programs try to avoid them from changing by political, cultural and economical transformations in order to prevent from decline in information collecting procedure. china is a distinct paradigm of such countries. Although most of china industries were damaged because of Cultural Revolution (1966-76) in 1970s but the satellite technology were excluded.

Causes for secretion of satellites systems

Satellites have advanced technology and yet their technology has not been assigned to countries extensively because of various causes. That is true that satellites are considered as tools for collecting information and such information can be used for political and military purposes. Therefore it can cause that one country overcome another. since the countries that lack it, may try to get it in order to attain secrets of other countries and monitor any movements from hostile or aggressive countries. In addition, exposure of satellite technology secrets will have crucial consequences for their owner, since addition of ability to fabricate the satellite by other countries; they can encounter their satellites.

Other than above considerations, if there would be countries that lack satellite technology, capable countries have opportunity in order to sell information with very high prices to developing countries and gain massively by this way. They can also compensate some of military information costs and even their economic expenses by selling information. The LAND SAT, NOAA, SPOT, satellites are good examples because they granted huge profits to US, Canada and France by extensive selling of information.

Role of satellite information in designing military operation

Application of satellite information in designing military operation has various dimensions that each one has its unique significance .Importance of these information depend on operation value and scale. Before operation, providing a view from battle field is required for focused information and analysis of operation area synchronically. Since the land condition is varied. Identifying it is very important. A located land in battlefield can be jungle or desert. That each one has its own major military conditions and characteristics. Determination of the characteristics by using of exact information is very reliable then other ways. In addition, the 3D images like MOMS can present a perfect image about phenomenon and make the way of operation designing very easier and exact. Thus all characteristics of a battlefield like plant coverage and angle of light irradiation can be stored and displayed as computer models and images. By using of satellite information, the validity of received information from various elements would be evaluated and they also can be used for easy comprehension of satellite images. In advanced phases, by investigating the satellites images and information at various periods, the information can be categorized and offered by its significance level or required time to operation designers and likewise, they could be informed about capabilities of enemy and earth and atmosphere situation.

Highways, airports, railways, food provision resources, fuel and water, each one has their special impacts on the warfare operation. Awareness about weakness and strength of enemy, economic talents, movements monitoring and having information about enemy defense method at critical time and even about enemy equipment capability are included as main items in using of satellite information for a good designing.

Using of satellite information in guarding from boundaries.

Using of apparatuses, identification missions, guarding from maritime and air forces, are included as process of information collecting and principal lookout at national security level. The national extensive information can include the collected information by above methods plus satellite information with low separablity to very high separablity and it can help to secure the territorial integrity. Satellites can do continual protecting operation from land, sea and space. The identifying and protecting operation by satellites, provide diverse information like aerologic, geographic, natural talents, transportation network and country manner while peacetime or wartime. such protection make possible the real-time alarming and warning about enemy actions.

Using of satellite information in designing the special operation

The especial operation are implemented and designed in asymmetric wars. such operation would be done at enemy deployment site or behind it. Forces with especial operation would be able to encounter with enemy operation. This kind of operation is very significant because of its information issues. If there is not possibility for constant access to targets position, the satellites can be used for examination of area. In one especial operation, the Information focus is more on strategic and operational targets and both long term and short-term impacts would be considered in this operation. The operation includes: invading to warfare communication lines of enemy and destructing of military facilities and industrial installations.

Examination of such positions on the satellite images would make possible the exact performance of operation at appropriate time. Determining the position of enemy unengaged forces and investigating of their talents and finding invasion ways, prepare the especial forces to destruct them. Such especial operations that are performed in especial sites are not often feasible without using of satellite information. KEN YORK the head clerk of TACTICAL TECHNOLOGY newsletter said: satellites assist to forces of especial operation in order to locate suitable areas for helicopters landing, people activities and etc.

Therefore the space plays a critical role throughout of special operation steps, from land large movements to hidden penetration of small parachutist groups or moving by helicopters.

Using of satellite information in strategic attacks

Today the warfare policy makers believe that space has added a fourth dimension to war.

2 policy makers in US during 1991 war said: the space has added fourth dimension to war and has affected on total path of attacks and save more people. Space alarms in launching of SCAT missiles. It provides a direction system with very high accuracy that considers tanks, missiles, airplanes and ships performance with details. Satellites identify targets, help people in order not to deal with sandstorm, indicate the soil moisture level and tell to forces commander SCHWARZKOPF in which parts of desert, tanks are able to move.

Strategic attacks make ascending effects on capability in war so that successful strategic attacks on critical areas of enemy can directly affect on its nation and allies. therefore if target selection is done exactly and attack impacts have is more its effect on war would be more. For example choosing a production center of nuclear electricity will be performed by using of images very convenient. Thus if one production unit of nuclear electricity is chosen among several ones and vital installations is considered inside it, the power production unit would be broke down by a small beat and since the level of its production is high, it would darken extensive area of a country. Its modifying and implementing will not be possible simply. Although such operation does not have an immediate impact on troops in front line but its impact on people and even authorities is very intensive. Definitely the air forces play the most important role in such operation. Not only they should assist to troops battling with enemy but also should attack on reserved forces or behind line troops from the air. The air forces need to satellite information more then all of other forces. Their mission is so that without satellite information, there will be no clear images from battlefield in their minds. whereas there is advanced systems in the world in order to make satellite images 3D and locate targets exactly by interpretation of satellite information, pilot would be able to attack his special targets with more accuracy in strategic invasions in order to avoid from flight recurring and damages that are caused by excessive presence of aircrafts on the strategic targets.

The effective activities for reaching to air excellence and attacking on enemy lines can reduce the power of enemy forces and prevent from its reinforcement and provide an opportunity for commanders to dominate by countermeasure.

By using of satellite images, areas can be controlled at nights and in cloudy weather. it enables pilots to use of any opportunity in order to attack enemy units or prevent its movements in frontlines and destruct any target any time.

Application of satellite images and information in land, maritime and air operations

I have attained a definite outcome in my studies about warfare operations. I realized that all warfare operations (even if a country lacks sea) are categorized to 3 categories: land, sea and air operations. Land, maritime and air forces have mission to guard from or attack to those areas. I tried to make a relationship between these 3 operations and satellites and I categorized the outcome to 3 parts.

Application of satellite information in land operation

Today the military usage of satellite images is categorized to several groups. Military designing are required to intelligence information to ensure the possibility of employing forces in an uncertain region. The more such information is exact and safe, will be more useful to hurt to enemy forces. Land regions always have been very important Indicating progress and withdrawing lines, locating the remote weapons, gathering information from safe sites, and food, water and equipment resources before operation are very important. It is required to detailed maps, awareness about nature and land from the view of transportation and identification of residents.

At age of cruise missile and intelligent bombs, it is required to earth details with 1 meter accuracy. Cruise missiles have intelligent systems that prevent from colliding to any natural or artificial barriers. Special targets to be attacked by such missiles are identified through satellites and the GPS satellites measure their coordinates. Target coordinates is defined in missile control system and missile would control its position by GPS satellites from launching time and in any moments, and move toward target that has its coordinates in the system. Because of owning the satellite control system, missiles are able to flee from anti missile and can return to initial orbit after height and orbit variation and never loose its target.

Awareness about enemy forces situation and military equipment and their placing type can be a good privilege. In face to face wars, such information should be included accurate location of commandoes and weapon secret sites.

With due to above points, the most important military and information application of satellites are:

1-   Climate forecasting and atmosphere studies

2-   detecting and positioning of enemy land forces and locating citadels and sites that enemy forces would gather there.

3-   Estimation of their talents from the view of forces and military equipment

4-   Verification and positioning of commands centers, bases and control centers of the enemy

5-   Land studies and earth examination for better transportation of forces and engineering

6-   Determination of military movements of enemy like forces, military equipment transportation and engineering activities.

7-   Examination of deployment situation and method of our forces and verification of our forces weaknesses, locating of penetrating sites and coordinating between forces.

8-   Accessing to position - related information and critical centers situation like bridges, communication paths, support centers, industrials and military strategic points in enemy behind lines.

9-   Determining the natural and artificial barriers like diged channels, mine fields, and concealment centers.

10-   Using of GPS system in directing and guiding forces

11-   Producing the PHOTOMAP for familiarity with operational region. In this method, the forces are able to examine the region situation exactly before entering to region.

12-   Using of operational region 3D images that has too many applications. For example measuring the declivity of region, roads or moonlight irradiance angle in order to move at night and also examine the region by method selection for building new bases.

13-   And finally examination of operation results and estimation of damages to enemy that is caused by land operation

Application of satellite information in maritime operation
Today the sea plays main role by advancing of maritime warfare systems and equipment expansion. Since sea makes possibility for accessing of involved countries to nearest contact line in shores and they even are able to enter their air and land forces to nearest contact line by sea. Employing the navy that carry aircraft has increased the role of navy during last years and has converted navy to multi roles and multi axis force. Accessing to warfare equipment technology in sea depth has highly enhanced the importance of maritime warfare. because forces, equipment and even strategic weapons can be approached to a country in sea depths so that they be hidden. Thus, even countries that no water boundaries have realized water operations. With due to above notes the most important applications of military satellite information in maritime operation are included:

1-   Weather studies and climate forecasting in specified time and place

2-   Ascertaining of maritime passageways and also examination of their width for determination of various floaters movement possibility by their weight and volume.

3-   Determination of natural barriers like seabed cliffs, shore and also sea residuals.

4-   Investigation of shore by geomorphology view and possibility of warfare and supporters ships to be sided and also examination of such shores for selecting suitable equipment in order to battle in shore and forces deployment there.

5-   Exact Identification of islands to be used in maritime operation or to be attacked.(an island usually can has many equipment for operation. such equipment are included light equipment, war forces provender, aircrafts and all type of missiles. Anyway satellite images can provide very exact images about enemy equipment and even the missile readiness situation in islands)

6-   Positioning the enemy and its diffusing and estimation of their talents

7-   Investigation of enemy movements including forces or warfare equipment on the sea

8-   Examination of our forces deployment and their weaknesses and strengths in islands, shores and sea.

9-   Determination of warm and cold flows of sea and sea surface temperature examination

10-   Measuring the ebbs and flows that would be done by nonmilitary and military satellites.

11-   Accessing to information about critical strategic centers situation of enemy both in sea and shore

12-	Measuring	sea	depth	and	shores	by BATHYMETER method(of course using of such depth meter by satellite information is a sensitive task and need to especial information and I think it is not very reliable for too deep regions)

13-	Examination of maritime barriers that is constructed by enemy like maritime minefield.

14-	Investigation of maritime operation outcomes and damages to enemy that is caused by maritime operation

15-	Deliberation of levels and types of contaminants that is caused by maritime warfare

Application of satellite information in air operation

As it is mentioned on pervious chapters, application of air forces is usually more effective in attack on depth and attacking to enemy forces can reduce their capabilities in place and time of invasion. The missions of air forces are tactical that assist to land or maritime operation directly. Such operations are included reciprocal air operation, supporting from own forces, especial operation of air transportation, identification, attack on strategic points and enemy communication lines that gives an opportunity to own commanders in order to dominate.

Air operations are very costly economically. The military operation is managed by an economic sense and while sequent attack on enemy; commanders should keep the finished price of their hardware low. While collecting static and information about destruction that is caused by air attack, it is highly required to spatial information.

Likewise not only using of satellite information creates the sufficient accuracy in attack on major points but also it would reduce the damages due to wasting of warfare equipment and weapons by choosing suitable methods.

With due to above notes, most important military applications of satellite information in air operation are:

1- Locating the important military and strategic points of enemy

2- Investigation of flight path by DTM (DIGITAL TERRAINE MODEL) provides flight possibility by very real vision from region in 3D method.

3- Forecasting the atmosphere phenomenon in air navigation

4- Launching the missile to specified targets

5- Investigation of flight path from the view of flight safety problems

6- Assessment of air operation and damages to enemy (in most of operations, assessment of damages while attacking is not possible. But some minutes and hours later the satellite images will help to assess damages or breaking down of attack site.

Eight principles of war and role of satellites

Although the war is a very bad way for solving problems and its harms would affect on people of countries but sometimes the war between 2 or more countries is inevitable.

In the most of military universities of the world, wars are based on some general principles in which satellite role is very important.

1-   Considering the attack by satellite

Aggressor forces usually begin their attack with air and missile invasions by using of attained information through satellites and to achieve crucial results in the war and then by using of satellite information and employed computers, continue their attack on major and strategic targets on enemy earth by intelligent missiles and aircrafts. And finally by land invasion, enter their forces to enemy country and occupy it. each one of above steps would be very difficult without satellites assistance.

2-   Considering the forces concentration by using of satellites.

In a war, because of required and immediate communication and coordination by aggressor countries, they are able to concentrate numerous forces during short time in operational region and dominate on enemy by using of less forces and their concentration in special points of enemy.

74

The principle of forces concentration that would be fulfilled easier by satellite, lead to force concentration in special time and place to achieve victory against enemy forces.

3-   Consideration of economizing in forces by using of satellites

Using of satellite information can assess deployment and reaction of enemy forces and with due to situation analysis; more forces can be used in especial regions and economize in using of forces. likewise it can be avoided from useless attacks by using of satellite information and economize in using of forces and warfare weapons.

4-   Considering the moving with fire principle by using of satellites

By using of satellite information in a war, the enemy military capability can be reduced by correct movements from forces and positioning them in a suitable situation than enemy forces and deployment of used missiles and other weapons in vulnerable points and involved forces can be used. Although doing such movements without satellite is feasible but it would be accompanied with very high errors and it is very difficult.

5-   Considering the principle of command unity by using of satellites

It is included 2 general categories: when several countries are battling with each other, the communication between several allied countries should be very regular and even one commander can be selected for several allied countries by their agreement. Any way they cannot be successful without organized communication with each other. The general commander or senior commanders are able to undertake the military communication and commanding bases of various allied forces by satellite systems and determines the required information and assigned missions to forces in the region and guide them by their commanding authority.

It doesn't matter that one country involves in war or several ones. Anyway there is a need to make some decisions far from war location. Satellites can gather specified information and send them to decision makers or commanders in commanding centers and guarantee an organized commanding center, incorporated communication control and command unity by this way.

6-   Considering the security principle by using of satellites

It depends on this fact, which a country is involved in war or is in peace. if a country is involved in war, it can control all enemy movements by using of satellites and be informed about it completely. It prevents own forces to be subjected against enemy forces.

Likewise if a country is not involved in war but is threatened constantly from one or more countries, it can identify the smallest variations on the earth surface and assess any variations in threatener countries forces and thus can maintain its security and prevent from subjection.

7- Considering the surprising principle by using of satellites

A country with high technology by parasiting in enemy protection system or bombing huge part of radars and demolishing of communication centers make impossible the reliable communication for enemy forces in order to disable their commanders to create substantial communication and consequently they can not surprise own forces by planning of suitable roles. On contrast, any country that has satellite system can control the enemy forces by using of satellites and surprise them.

8- Considering the principle of simply by using of satellites

As it is described in simply principle aggressor forces should be able to recognize the assigned missions by their commanders in order to implement them correctly.

The communication satellites can establish the connection between commanders and their subsystem elements easily, and aggressor forces can locate their position by using of GPS systems in any moment and know they are located in which coordinates than other forces. Thus by using of above system, other similar equipment are able to perform assigned missions easily and recognize the military missions because of their high military knowledge and delivering such missions is not very difficult and complex for them.

Conclusion

Few years ago and according to advancing of human scientific tools, although struggle in controlling of space for nonmilitary applications along with exploring in space for military objectives has been increased and often distinguishing between military and nonmilitary objective has been difficult but it is definite that such scientific tools play a main role in solving all problems of a country. So the powerful countries without their military satellites will not have their real potential and the economic powerful countries also have dependency to their nonmilitary satellites. Of course they are beholden to military satellites for guarding from their economy. In this pressuring competition of technology, intelligence agencies across the world pay attention to economic and technologic information and military satellite systems that make possible to control opponents by photographing, overhearing or other ways and are used as weapons in economic and military war. Because of critical role of military satellite, information about them are secret and most of people even don't know their names while they provide very especial information for people of the world. for example the VELA 12 has shown good capabilities in recording the nuclear explosions so that it recorded a nuclear explosion in south Africa in 22 September of 1979 casually and it was considered on top main news for a long time, or the American 647 satellite has measurer system that it determines distant range missiles or their spatial spaceship riser reactors and telecommunicate to land terminals DENVER in Colorado and ALICE SPRING in Australia. Such satellites and P-1-8 satellite owe very strong measurer which can control the situation of CRUISE missiles, airplanes, land to land missiles, land to earth missiles, air to land missiles and distant rang missiles.

Using of some nonmilitary satellite information with high quality can also expose the hidden nuclear equipment. it is able to show Anti Aircraft weapons, resistant shelters of nuclear weapons stores and special bombs, stores of nuclear fuel. like images that had been taken from Israel nuclear installation in 1991 in DIMONA by SPOT satellite. it indicated that installation of plutonium decomposition may be exist there. But any way military satellites act strongly even in this field.

But role of military satellites has been increased after 1990s years and gulf war. Because the spatial military machines of US in 1991 war could be named as real victor. The KH 11 satellite for taking extra clear photos from space, totally secret satellites as MAGNUM for hearing external telephone conversations, LACROSSE satellites for gathering produced photos by radar waves from foreign climes, highly secret JUMPSEAT satellites for discovering the electronic telecommunication, were nice proofs to confirm this.

it has never been seen in history that an army bet so on consequences that occur faraway from earth.